BRITAIN IN Ol

# CRYSTAL PALACE, PENGE AND ANERLEY

An aerial view of the Crystal Palace looking towards the Parade and the high-level station, *c*. 1930.

BRITAIN IN OLD PHOTOGRAPHS

# CRYSTAL PALACE, PENGE AND ANERLEY

*MICK SCOTT*

BROMLEY LIBRARIES AND MUSEUMS SERVICE

ALAN SUTTON PUBLISHING LIMITED

Alan Sutton Publishing Limited
Phoenix Mill · Far Thrupp · Stroud
Gloucestershire · GL5 2BU

First published 1995

Copyright © Mick Scott, 1995

*Cover photograph*: Penge tramways official
inspection at the Crystal Palace, April 1906.
*Title page*: the Crystal Palace from the
Belvedere Road area.

**British Library Cataloguing in Publication Data.**
A catalogue record for this book is available from
the British Library.

ISBN 0-7509-0694-4

Typeset in 9/10 Sabon.
Typesetting and origination by
Alan Sutton Publishing Limited.
Printed in Great Britain by
Ebenezer Baylis, Worcester.

The first motorcycle race was held at the Crystal Palace in 1926. For a period between 1929 and 1934 the Glaziers Speedway Team held meetings at the Palace. In 1937 the first motor-car race was held on the specially created racetrack. These are competitors in a midget car race.

# Contents

A Whit Monday race meeting, 1955. A racetrack so close to London was very popular. However, high speeds, increased safety standards and noise finally forced the circuit to close in August 1972. During the short time it was in operation, motor racing greats such as Roy Salvadori, Mike Hawthorn, Stirling Moss, Jack Brabham, Graham Hill, James Hunt, Jackie Stewart, Jochen Rindt and Emerson Fittipaldi raced here.

The main and south entrance to the Crystal Palace. Note the taxi ranks and the railway line.

# *Acknowledgements*

I acknowledge with thanks the work of the Crystal Palace Foundation, the Crystal Palace Museum, Patrick Beaver, Doris Pullen, Graham Reeves and Alan Warwick. The photographs are from the Local Studies Collection of the Bromley Libraries and Museums Service, and I would like to thank the Local Studies staff for their patience while I was working on this book. I would like to thank Mr Kenneth Talbot for allowing me to reproduce the photographs taken by the Crystal Palace photographer, Arthur Talbot. This book is for my parents and the others of their generation who can say 'I saw the Crystal Palace burn down'.

# Introduction

Penge and Anerley are part of the London Borough of Bromley. They are the most urbanized parts of the borough, and they are less than 10 miles from the centre of London.

Penge dates back to the ninth century as a detached hamlet of the parish of Battersea, and it remained part of the county of Surrey until the end of the nineteenth century. In 1067 it was granted, with Battersea, to the abbot of Westminster. In the Domesday Book it is mentioned as 'a wood for 50 hogs pannage'. Pannage was a duty paid to the manorial lord for the right to graze pigs in the wood, and it is possible that from the word pannage we get Penge. Penge remained as a rural hamlet until, in 1801, the Croydon canal was cut across Penge Common. In 1839 the railway engineer Joseph Gibbs used much of the canal basin for his railway.

Anerley was the name given to a solitary house on Penge Common not far from the Robin Hood public house, a notorious haunt for highwaymen. The house was owned by a Scot, William Sanderson, who gave it the name because it was the 'ainley' house in the area. He offered land to the South Eastern Railway in return for a guarantee that a station would be built at Anerley. In 1839 the line was opened with stations at Anerley and Penge.

Thus Penge and Anerley were among the first districts in the area to benefit from the railway, and they became fashionable suburbs of London, especially after the Crystal Palace was re-erected nearby. One of their earliest claims to fame dates from 1846 when Edward Lear published the following limerick in his *Book of Nonsense*:

> There was an old person of Anerley,
> Whose conduct was strange and unmannerly;
> He rushed down the Strand with a pig in each hand,
> But returned in the evening to Anerley.

The story of the Crystal Palace begins in 1850. Prince Albert had organized a series of successful industrial exhibitions with his collaborator Henry Cole. He decided that in 1851 they would organize their biggest yet, a British Exhibition of National Design and Manufacture. The first intention was to hold the exhibition in Somerset House. The prince then decided that the exhibition must embrace foreign products, and it was realized that a much larger venue was needed. The idea of a temporary building in Hyde Park was mooted. A Royal Commission was appointed to raise money for the building and to organize a competition for a suitable design. Despite several entries, no choice was made. Time was running out when Joseph Paxton, a landscape gardener, submitted a rough drawing made on a piece of blotting paper of an enormous conservatory. The design was accepted and Paxton completed the plans in nine days.

In August 1850, with nine months to go to the opening of the exhibition, the foundations were laid in Hyde Park. The building contained 4,500 tons of iron, 293,655 sheets of glass and was 1,848 ft long, 408 ft wide and 108 ft at its tallest point.

On 1 May 1851 Queen Victoria formally opened the Great Exhibition. By the time it closed in October, over six million people had visited the building. Many travelled hundreds of miles to do so, and it is reported that one old woman walked from Cornwall to see the sights. For the first time large numbers of people from all walks of life were encouraged to congregate together, working men took holidays to see the exhibition, and the importance of the railway network for transporting so many visitors was clearly seen. The exhibition was also financially successful – it made £180,000 profit. This sum was used to endow many of the institutions that we take for granted today, such as the Kensington museums.

Once the exhibition had closed, it was necessary to decide what would happen to the building. Paxton, now Sir Joseph, wanted it to remain in Hyde Park as a winter garden, but Parliament ruled that it should be demolished. Paxton had an alternative plan. He formed the Crystal Palace Company and, by selling shares, raised £500,000. He purchased the Crystal Palace for £70,000 and Penge Place for £50,000. Then he set about rebuilding the palace at Penge. No expense was spared and the costs were so crippling that the Crystal Palace never made money. The fountains were designed to rival those at Versailles and required tremendous water pressure to operate. Attempts to build two water towers failed, and when water tanks were placed on the wings of the building the glass cracked ominously. It took Isambard Kingdom Brunel to find the answer – a pair of 200 ft towers that flanked the palace until the Second World War. The palace was an enormous popular success and every type of entertainment was presented here, from symphony concerts to pantomime and from aqua shows to bicycle polo. The palace drew people like a magnet to live in the area, men like the painter Camille Pissarro and the composer Arthur Sullivan worked in the vicinity, and it brought activity and prosperity to the districts that surrounded it. When it was destroyed it left an enormous gap in the life of this part of south London which is as yet unfilled.

Today the Crystal Palace is managed by the Leisure and Community Service of the London Borough of Bromley, which is slowly reviving one of the largest parks in Greater London. Two organizations are based at the palace. One, the Crystal Palace Foundation, exists to promote research and education on the palace, together with the conservation of some of the historic parts of the site. The other, the Crystal Palace Museum, is housed in the only surviving building constructed by the Crystal Palace Company, which was erected in 1872 as a school for practical engineering. The museum tells the story of the Crystal Palace through displays and exhibits.

These photographs of Penge, Anerley and the Crystal Palace are part of the extensive Local Studies Collection of books, maps, newspapers, ephemera and other archives held at Bromley Central Library. It is a collection which grows in importance, and I am fortunate to have it in my care.

Mick Scott
Senior Librarian, Local Studies
Bromley Libraries and Museums Service

*Section One*

# PENGE AND ANERLEY

*The children's corner at Penge Recreation Ground.*

The Triangle. Penge.

The Crooked Billet is reputed to be the oldest established inn in Penge, an area that is not short of a public house or two, and dates from 1792. The Crooked Billet took its name from a curiously shaped billet cut with a billhook from a tree outside the inn, and for many years preserved in the bar. The first coaching inn was a wooden structure with a small tea garden and a wooden staircase outside leading to the first floor. It served the travellers on the old coach road between Beckenham and Dulwich. It was demolished and the almshouses built on the site, and the second inn was built on its current site on the opposite side of the road in 1840. As Penge grew, the Crooked Billet was enlarged and became the regular meeting place of the Masons, the Druids, the British Legion, the Oddfellows and the Penge Hearts of Oak Slate Club.

The Penge Triangle was the site of an ancient oak tree. Under the tree was a seat, which was a popular place for locals to sit and talk.

On 22 October 1809 the Croydon Canal was opened to join Croydon to the River Thames via the Grand Surrey Canal. Built at a cost of £148,000, it ran through New Cross, Forest Hill and Sydenham, then crossed Penge Common and proceeded towards Selhurst Wood and Croydon. The intention was to provide safe transport for goods through to the south of England without passage by sea, which at the time of the Napoleonic Wars was highly dangerous. Common cargoes included timber, stone, brick, chalk, clay and dung.

The canal was never a profitable concern and in 1836 it was finally sold to the Croydon Railway Company. This stretch in Betts Park and the man-made lake at South Norwood are all that is left of the canal.

As the fortune of the canal declined, so considerable interest was shown by developers in building a railway from London to Croydon. In 1835 an Act of Parliament was granted to the London and Croydon Railway Company for a line. The company saw the possibility of following the route of the canal and in 1836 purchased the canal for £40,250. The railway opened in 1839 at a total outlay of £528,000 and for some distance its route lies in the bed of the canal. There was originally a level-crossing at Penge, where a policeman attended to the gates. Trains were timed to reach London in 26 minutes and the fares were 1s 3d first class, 1s second and 9d third.

When the railway was being constructed, William Sanderson, a Scot, offered part of his land at Penge without charge provided that a station was built on the land and called Anerley. A local directory for 1859 records that there was a hotel and tea gardens adjoining Anerley Station but 'there is no place of that name'. The Anerley Gardens were opened in 1841 and comprised a rustic Swiss Cottage, a bandstand and a maze. These were closed in 1868 when competition from the Crystal Palace became too intense. The railway company advertised fishing in the canal as an added attraction.

Kent House Farm, c. 1907. The origins of Kent House can be traced back to the thirteenth century. In the late eighteenth century the house was owned by John Julius Angerstein, the founder of Lloyds of London. In the nineteenth century Kent House was a farm which consisted of 178 acres in 1869. The house was used as a nursing home and as a hotel before being demolished.

The Watermen and Lightermen's Almshouses, *c.* 1890. In the early part of Queen Victoria's reign a number of bridges were built over the River Thames. This caused hardship to many of the men who worked on the river. To alleviate some of the distress, the Company of Watermen and Lightermen of the River Thames set up a committee to erect almshouses for the 'poor, aged, decayed and maimed' freemen of the company. Mr J. Dudin Brown of Sydenham gave 2 acres of land at Penge for the site. Queen Adelaide agreed to be patroness of the almshouses and gave a gift of £100. The foundation stone was laid by the Lord Mayor of London on Saturday 16 May 1840. The building, designed in the popular Tudor style and built by George Porter, comprised 48 houses each with three rooms, an outside toilet and water from a well. The first residents moved in on 4 November 1841. A master, matron and gatekeeper were appointed to look after the inmates, and were expected to leave if they became infirm. The almshouses were the first substantial buildings in the area.

In 1973 the residents moved to new premises in Hastings and the buildings were modernized and reoccupied. This photograph of the gardens was taken in 1967.

The Watermen's Almshouses at the Crooked Billet, Penge. This is one of many picture postcards of the area.

St John's Church was erected on land given by the Watermen and Lightermen's Company to provide a church for the inhabitants of their asylum and the people of Penge Common. Erected in 1849, the church was built of stone in the Gothic style. The tower and spire contained a clock and six bells.

The interior of St John's Church.

High Street, *c.* 1910. A tram is passing the almshouses.

King William IV's Naval Asylum was founded in 1849 by Queen Adelaide as a memorial to her husband William, Queen Victoria's uncle. The building was intended for the widows of twelve serving naval officers. The queen was very concerned about the welfare of the navy and left instructions that on her death she should be carried to her grave by sailors. She is buried at Windsor.

The Naval Asylum was designed by Philip Hardwick in a mock Tudor style popular for almshouse construction in the nineteenth century. It consists of a series of cottages that form a quadrangle, the space enclosed being laid out as a garden.

The Queen Adelaide public house still stands in Penge High Street, opposite the almshouses. The church across the road was to provide for the inmates' spiritual needs; perhaps the pub catered for their more earthly ones!

In 1855 the Metropolitan Management Act was passed to try to regulate the local government of London at that time. Under this Act, Penge was transferred from Battersea to the Lewisham Board and most district matters were managed by the Penge Vestry. The vestry men were elected in much the same way that councillors are today. The vestry met in various places, including church halls, private houses and even public houses, until in 1879 it moved into the newly built Vestry Hall.

In 1899 the London Government Act was passed, under which Penge became part of Kent; this led in 1900 to the formation of the Penge Urban District Council. The first meeting was held on Friday 9 November 1900 in Anerley Town Hall.

The Town Hall in Anerley Road was opened in 1879. It is a building of white brick with Bath stone dressing and has a turret containing an illuminated clock. It housed the offices of the Clerk of the Council, rate collectors, surveyors and public health officials. There were also committee rooms, and two large halls for public meetings and entertainments. In 1911 the property was enlarged and a new council chamber was built. The building is still in use and today it houses Anerley Library.

*Opposite*: Penge Fire Station, Croydon Road, *c.* 1910. Penge Urban District Council took over responsibility for the fire brigade from the London County Council in 1901. There were two fire stations: one at the Town Hall and one in Beckenham Road. A horse-powered fire-engine with hose and harness was purchased in 1902 from Messrs Merryweather and Son for £179 2s 2d, and arrangements were made to stable the horses at the premises of Thomas Tillings at the Pawleyne Arms. Tillings provided a driver when needed, and an electric bell was fixed to the stable so that the stableman could have the horses harnessed and brought to the fire station when there was a call. This building was erected at the depot site and was first occupied in July 1910. In 1911 a motor fire-engine was purchased from Merryweathers. It was the Penge Fire Brigade that first answered the call to the Crystal Palace in 1936.

Council chamber, Anerley Town Hall.

Penge police station, *c.* 1905. A temporary station was first opened in Penge in April 1870 following public demand for a police presence in the hamlet. In 1869 Mr William Gibson of the parochial council wrote to the Metropolitan Commissioner: 'A police station should be erected with the coming of winter and consequently an increase in crime, on the growth in poverty and want of employment of the lower classes in the locality.' The current police station was built in about 1872 and is one of the oldest in the Metropolitan area.

The Public Library Act was adopted in Penge in 1891. A temporary reading room was opened in Station Road in Anerley in 1892. This building in Oakfield Road was opened by Sir J. Blundell Maple on 1 July 1899 and was to serve as the library for many years.

The library, decorated for the coronation of King Edward VII in 1902.

Penge Tramways official inspection at the Crystal Palace, April 1906. The South Metropolitan Electric Tramways and Lighting Company completed the construction of a line from the Croydon boundary at Selby Road to Penge in that month. The line was extended to the Crystal Palace by May. However, the inspector insisted that only experienced drivers should be allowed to take the trams up Anerley Hill and that special brakes would be fitted, which effectively drove a spike into the track if there was a danger of a runaway tram.

Penge Recreation Ground was opened on 4 July 1888. A procession through Penge preceded a service of prayers. The Crystal Palace fire-engine followed the procession and more than a thousand children lined the route. The land was originally purchased by the Lewisham Board of Works in 1887 with the intention of providing gravel for road building. St John's Church is in the background.

The drinking fountain was presented to the Lewisham Board of Works by Mrs Blundell Maple, the wife of the member for Dulwich. Mrs Maple turned on the tap to take the first drink.

The gates to the recreation ground, decorated for the coronation of King Edward VII in 1902.

The children's corner at the recreation ground.

The drinking fountain in Alexandra Road Recreation Ground. The Recreation Ground was in the Beckenham Borough but was laid out towards the end of the nineteenth century on part of the old Penge cricket ground. It was extended to 11 acres in 1911.

A bandstand was constructed on Alexandra Road Recreation Ground in 1905.

Road safety lessons in Alexandra Road Recreation Ground.

The Penge Chapel was built in 1837 to provide for the large number of people who wished to worship in Penge. The initial cost was £416 10s, and the chapel was built on land at the corner of Croydon Road and the High Street, which was purchased from Albert Cator for £35. A new church, St John's, was opened in 1849 and in 1850 the chapel was converted to St John's school. It remained a school until it was demolished in 1937.

A boys' class with Mr Champ, the headmaster of St John's National School for Boys, 1928.

Beckenham and Penge County School for Boys, *c.* 1930. Founded in 1901, this new building, which was designed by Major W.H. Robinson, FRIBA, at a cost of £50,000, was opened in 1931. It was built to accommodate 510 pupils.

The large hall, Beckenham and Penge County School, *c.* 1930.

The woodwork shop, Beckenham and Penge County School, *c.* 1930.

The Penge and Beckenham Co-operative Society building in Green Lane.

High Street, looking east with the police station on the left and the Congregational Chapel on the right.

High Street, Penge.

The Central Exchange was a parade of shops built on the corner of Beckenham Road and Green Lane in 1899. Lilley and Skinner, bootmakers, was one of the earliest shops to take space here.

High Street, *c.* 1950. Woolworths occupied Nos 147–151 with Williamson's restaurant next door.

Pickfords, Nos 143–151 Beckenham Road, were described in the 1910 directory as 'carriers'; however, they were to develop into a removal and travel agents, and at this time were offering trips to Paris and Swanage.

Beckenham Road, at the corner of Southey Street, Penge, c. 1910. Arthur Richardson, the butcher, is displaying carcasses in the open. The Watermen's Arms public house is in the middle distance.

Beckenham Road, *c.* 1920. Croydon Road is on the left with the police station on the right. The roof of the Penge Empire can be seen in the background. Note the tramlines and overhead power cables.

Flooding in Beckenham Road, Whit Sunday 1897.

The site for the Penge Empire in 1914.

The Empire Theatre, Penge, at the corner of Clarina Road and the High Street, opened on 3 April 1915 with a special gala featuring Marie Lloyd. In 1949 the building became the Essoldo Cinema. It was then demolished in 1960. During its lifetime, many stars of music hall and variety played here, including Flanagan and Allen, Wee Georgie Wood, G.H. Elliot, and Jack Hylton, as well as actors such as Alec McCowen, Hugh Paddick, Noel Gordon and Denholm Elliot. Local residents still recall seeing Max Miller at the Empire playing second on the bill to Larry Adler.

Penge Conservative and Unionist Club, situated at 22–24 Beckenham Road.

Crystal Palace Park Road, *c.* 1900. A road of fashionable houses was built after the construction of the Crystal Palace for those who wished to live in its shadow.

Oakfield Road was one of the first to be developed in the area. By 1910 it was a prosperous mixture of shops and houses.

A leafy cul-de-sac of town houses built in the 1860s, Avington Grove was typical of buildings in the area following the construction of the Crystal Palace.

The Penge entrance gate to the Crystal Palace. This shed was rather less imposing than the grand entrance at the Parade.

The railway bridge at the Penge entrance to the Crystal Palace.

Members of the Penge Salvation Army Boy Scouts collecting for the Prince of Wales' National Relief Fund.

The Penge war memorial. A Celtic cross at the Beckenham Road entrance to the recreation ground was erected by C.E. Ebbutt's of Croydon at a cost of £237 10s, to be paid by the War Memorial Fund. The memorial was unveiled by the chairman of the council on Sunday 25 September 1921 at 3.00 p.m. More than 4,000 copies of the order of service were distributed by Scouts, and the last post was sounded by buglers and drums of the 5th Battalion Royal West Kent Regiment. In the photograph the Revd I. Near is giving a short address.

The scene after the ceremony.

Street celebrations in Maple Road, 1930s.

Penge War Weapons Week, 19–26 April 1941. The procession is passing the Crooked Billet and the Watermen's Almshouses.

Members of the Auxiliary Fire Service in the War Weapons Week Parade.

Street collectors for War Weapons Week. The organ grinder was a common sight locally.

Maple Road was the main link between Penge and Anerley and was developed before Croydon Road. This area was laid out in a grid system and each house had a garden. The roads were all named after plants and trees. As well as Maple there was Laurel, Woodbine, Hawthorn and Jasmine linked at the north by Oakfield Road. Jasmine Road was originally known by its older spelling of Jessamine.

Maple Road.

Maple Road.

The corner of Maple Road and Laurel Grove. The Baptist Tabernacle, erected in 1893 on the site of an earlier building of 1867, could seat 1,130 people.

The Baptist Tabernacle.

Looking down Anerley Road, showing the way the houses and shops spread along the main road from Anerley Station to the Crystal Palace.

A tram in Anerley Road.

The London and Provincial Bank Ltd at the corner of Anerley Road and Station Road. On the other corner were the premises of Walford and Wilshin, estate agents.

The London and South Western Bank in Anerley Road, looking towards the railway station. These two postcards were produced before (top) and after (bottom) the construction of the tramway in 1906.

Anerley Road.

Looking up Anerley Road.

Looking up Anerley Road towards the water-tower, *c.* 1900.

Anerley Congregational Church was opened on 20 January 1876 and replaced an older church in Jasmine Grove. It was built of Bath stone and red brick, and it seated 1,170 people. The spire was 150 ft high.

The Congregational Church, Anerley, *c.* 1900.

Holy Trinity Church, on the corner of Anerley Road and Croydon Road, was built in 1872 with money raised from the public. It was a brick building with stone dressing. The church was badly damaged by bombs during the Second World War and was subsequently demolished.

The interior of Holy Trinity Church, Anerley.

Anerley railway station.

Thicket Road, Anerley.

Thicket Road, Anerley.

The Thicket Road entrance to the Crystal Palace.

The Thicket Hotel, Anerley Road. This public house features in the 1871 directory.

The North Surrey District School, situated in Anerley Road, was built in 1847 by the Poor Law Unions of Lewisham, Wandsworth and Reigate. In these stark buildings the children of the poor were educated in technical subjects and were taught a trade, the aim being to make them self-supporting. It was a large brick building standing in 7 acres of ground with its own farm and kitchen garden. The children lived in fourteen dormitories.

In later years the building was used as a residential home for elderly men who worked in nurseries growing flowers for market. The building was demolished in the 1950s.

A garden party at the Holy Trinity vicarage, No. 194 Anerley Road. This building became the public library.

The Brooklyn Nursing Institute was a private nursing home for paying patients in Anerley Road.

Looking down Anerley Hill from the top, a tram can be seen making the laborious ascent.

Croydon Road, Anerley. A horse bus is passing the Mitre public house near the Croydon boundary.

The Rising Sun public house, on the left opposite the clock.

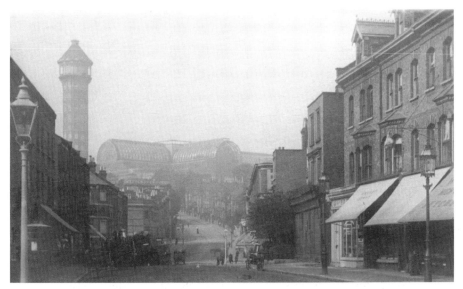

The Crystal Palace from Anerley Road.

The Crystal Palace from Anerley Road, *c.* 1900. The entrance to the Crystal Palace low-level station is to the right.

The Crystal Palace from Anerley Road.

An aerial view of Penge with the High Street and St John's Church in the centre, *c*. 1920.

# THE CRYSTAL PALACE

# 1854–1936

*A bull with a man's head,*

*from the Assyrian court.*

Once the Great Exhibition in Hyde Park had closed the building was dismantled, and the sections and glass panels were numbered and brought to Penge Place by horse and cart. On 5 August 1852 a ceremony was held to plant the first column.

The Crystal Palace under construction in 1852. The new Crystal Palace took almost two years to complete. It was enlarged to include transepts and wings at the north and south ends. It was both wider and taller than the original, with an arched roof rising above it.

Over 5,000 men worked on the rebuilding. These men were known as 'navigators' or 'navvies' and came from all over the country. A large number of them lived in a walled estate called Norwood New Town. This area became infamous for fighting between drunken men, and police patrolled the outside to keep any intoxicated workmen within. In 1854 over a thousand navvies formed the Army Works Corps and went to dig trenches in the Crimea.

As in the original, every new technological advancement available was used in the rebuilding. Mass-production and off-site fabrication were used to the full. Throughout the building, every horizontal measurement was a multiple of 8 ft. This method readily lent itself to the partitioning of the area into courts. The centre transept was 120 ft wide (15 x 8) while the height was 168 ft (21 x 8). Overall the building was 1,600 ft long by 300 ft wide. Despite the care taken, there was an incident when scaffolding collapsed in the great transept and twelve men were killed.

The central transept. This photograph demonstrates the method of construction of the
Crystal Palace and its subsequent light airy feel. Notice the construction of the dais for
the opening ceremony of 10 June 1834 which was attended by Queen Victoria. This
grand event was recorded as follows: 'In spite of her worries and preoccupations
connected with the impending outbreak of the Crimean War, Her Majesty looked as
radiant as the summer weather with which the ceremony was blessed. The inauguration
was witnessed by 40,000 people, including the Lord Mayor of London. A guard of
honour round the throne was formed by the Coldstream Guards and the Honourable
Artillery Company, the national anthem was rendered in a most impressive manner by a
chorus of 400 instrumentalists, 200 vocal performers and two regimental bands besides
the special Palace Band – the whole under the leadership of Signor Costa. The solo parts
were sung by Madame Clara Novello.' (*Crystal Palace Sale Particular*, 1911)

On either side of the northern portion of the nave was a series of fine art courts containing facsimiles of the remains of the architecture and sculpture of various periods. The intention was to give the untravelled visitor the same advantages as the privileged traveller. The English medieval court contained four tombs, those of Edward the Black Prince, Edward II, his mother Eleanor and William of Wykeham, together with examples of architecture from Rochester and Lincoln cathedrals. The medieval court, by Augustus Pugin, had been a feature of the Great Exhibition and was joined at the Crystal Palace by a number of other courts.

The north nave. Further along the nave, to left and right behind the shrubs and statues, appeared the walls of the fine art courts.

The crystal fountain in the south transept was a feature of the Great Exhibition at Hyde Park and was brought to Sydenham with the building. It was made by Osler and included two basins, canopies, pinnacles, columns and buttresses on serrated and fluted bases in cut glass.

The tropical department was kept at a temperature of 70° Fahrenheit and housed palms, ferns and bamboos. A collection of foreign birds, including parrots, cockatoos and love-birds, was kept in an aviary here.

The Elizabethan court featured effigies of Elizabeth and Mary Queen of Scots, as well as a bust of Shakespeare. The architectural details were copied from Holland House in London.

The Greek court contained a model of the Parthenon and a copy of the Venus de Milo. This photograph was taken before June 1854 when, after a letter was received from 'thirteen eminent persons', the male figures were emasculated by a workman with a chisel, and fig leaves attached instead.

Painting the Colossus of Abu Simbel in the Egyptian court in 1854. These enormous figures were cast on the site.

The Egyptian court was the most magnificent of the 120 courts and included pillars from the temple at Karnak and these figures of Rameses II.

The Egyptian court.

The tomb of Giuliano de Medici in the Italian court. This court was later converted to the Crystal Palace Club.

The Assyrian court and Ninevah court, with the human-headed bulls of Khorsabad.

The Assyrian court was destroyed by the fire of 1866 and was never replaced.

Figures from the poem 'Tam O'Shanter', by Robert Burns.

The Crystal Palace, showing the north transept destroyed by the fire of 1866. This photograph is by Negretti and Zambra.

The north transept, tower and Italian gardens. The Italian gardens, including ornamental fountains, temples and cascades, were designed and laid out by Sir Joseph Paxton. The English landscape gardens included winding walks, pleasant slopes and gentle undulations. From the stairs, in the distance the churches of Penge, Beckenham, Bickley and Bromley, and even the Knockholt Beeches, formed a perfect panorama.

The Italian gardens and north tower, with the orangery in the background. Sir Joseph Paxton purchased 110 orange and pomegranate trees when the property of the Orleans family of France was sold by public auction. Some of the trees were four hundred years old.

North tower, north end and the upper archery ground. 'On an extensive slope which is bordered in the distance by a bank of shrubs is the Archery and Croquet Ground most picturesquely situated, and, from its natural position, admirably adapted to this purpose. A range of targets is placed at various distances, and an extensive assortment of bows, arrows, etc. as well as all the appliances for playing croquet, may be obtained for the use of visitors by application to the attendant constantly on the spot.' (*Crystal Palace: Illustrated Guide to the Palace and Park*, 1893.)

The Crystal Palace before the fire of 1866.

The grounds from the upper terrace.

The north transept. This is one of a set of three postcards issued for the Jubilee celebration.

The north tower and orangery. This photograph shows the north wing before it was destroyed in the gales of 1861. Many years later the area occupied by the square tower became the dancing platform.

Looking over the fountains from the terraces. On the right is a brick and iron building of sixteen sides with a domed roof, in which was displayed the panorama painted by M. Philippoteaux.

The lower lake of 5¾ acres was devoted to water activities and in the winter to ice-skating. The artesian well that fed this lake and subsequently all of the intermediate lakes and fountains was more than 575 ft deep. The lower lake was known as the tidal lake because the depth of water decreased as it was pumped to the upper reservoir at night and then increased as the water flowed back into it during the day.

The rosary consisted of 120 latticework columns supporting twelve arches covered in roses. This was later the site for Hiram Maxim's flying machine.

Using the best information available at the time, the 'monsters' were created as the Crystal Palace was being built. Constructed of brick, iron and concrete, they caused a sensation, being discussed in the press and visited by Queen Victoria; the mould of the Iguanodon was used as seating for a dinner held on New Year's Eve, 1853. Waterhouse Hawkins, the designer, hosted the event which was held to entertan eminent scholars.

The prehistoric monsters. The area around the lower lake, with access by a rustic bridge, was one of the most interesting sections of the Crystal Palace. The 1893 guide states: 'It is here that one of the most original features of the Crystal Palace Company's grand plan of visual education has been carried out. There, all the leading features of Geology are found displayed in so practical and popular a manner that a child may discern the characteristic points of that truly useful branch of the history of nature. The spectator standing on the upper terrace of the plateau has before him the largest educational model ever attempted in any part of the world. . . . All of the models of restored forms of extinct animals were designed, modelled and constructed by Mr Waterhouse Hawkins, aided by the counsel and criticism of Professor Owen.' (*Crystal Palace: Illustrated Guide to the Palace and Park*, 1893.)

Two women pose with one of the prehistoric creatures on the antediluvian island. The island has been visited by countless children. The reconstructed animals are now officially listed and in the care of the London Borough of Bromley. This photograph was taken by the Crystal Palace Company photographer, Arthur Talbot.

'Prehistoric Peeps'.

The Crystal Palace from the grounds.

The School of Art, Science and Literature was set up in 1859 to give an educational vitality to the collections. 'The plan embraces systematic tuition in the manner of private tutorial instruction by masters and professors of the highest status, at fees fixed as moderately as may be found possible.' (*Crystal Palace Sale Particular*, 1911)

The School of Practical Engineering was set up in 1872 by Mr J.W. Wilson, who had worked in both the 1851 Exhibition and the re-erection of the Crystal Palace in 1854. The school was located in the south tower.

The Crystal Palace, looking towards the cab rank at the top of Anerley Hill, *c.* 1900. 'By road the journey is delightful. The route from Charing Cross is by Vauxhall Bridge, Brixton and Norwood; and from the City by Camberwell and Dulwich; the distance in either case is under eight miles. The Company's stables are situated within three minutes' walk of the Central Transept Entrance, where every accommodation can be obtained.' (*Crystal Palace: Illustrated Guide to the Palace and Park*, 1893.)

The Crystal Palace Parade, *c.* 1900. The White Swan public house is on the left.

Crystal Palace Parade, looking north-east, 1914.

The Parade, a popular area to promenade in one's Sunday best. The Parade was painted by Camille Pissarro, a French impressionist painter who lived and painted in the area between 1871 and 1872.

The main entrance on the Crystal Palace Parade, looking north-east.

The Crystal Palace, from a postcard.

The Crystal Palace, showing the glass-covered railway colonnade from the low-level station.

The low-level station. Paxton had realized how important the railway would be to the project and this line was specifically built for passengers travelling on the London and Brighton Railway from London Bridge and Victoria. The station and line were opened on 10 June 1854. The owner of the site, Penge Place, was Leo Schuster, a director of the London and Brighton Railway. A special line was constructed from the Jolly Sailor Station, later Norwood Junction, to bring building materials to the site.

On 1 August 1865 the London, Chatham and Dover Railway opened its branch line from Peckham Rye to the high-level station alongside the Crystal Palace Parade. A subway connected the station to the palace, and Italian craftsmen were commissioned to build the vaulted brickwork of the subway. This can still be seen today. In 1893 the first class return fare from London Bridge, including the admission fee, was 2s 6d.

Music played a very important part in the life of the Crystal Palace. Paxton had not envisaged the Crystal Palace as a place for concerts, but a small German band played in the transepts at regular intervals. In 1855 August Manns was appointed Director of Music, and with the enthusiastic support of the Crystal Palace secretary, George Grove, a full orchestra was engaged and played daily concerts. The main concert of the week was on a Saturday, and crowds flocked from the metropolis to attend. Manns featured the works of less well-known composers, such as Schumann and Schubert, and in 1862 Arthur Sullivan's first work, the music to Shakespeare's *The Tempest*, was given its premiere. Later George Grove appointed Sullivan professor of pianoforte and ballad singing at the Crystal Palace School of Art.

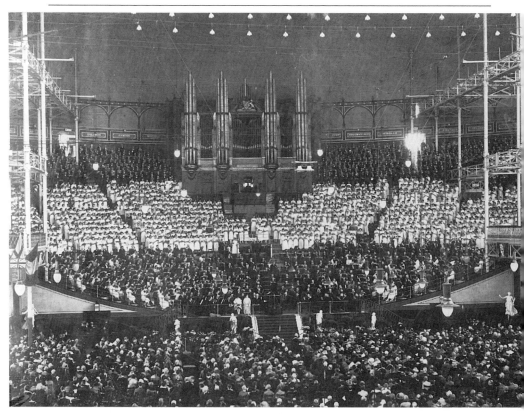

The Handel Festival, June 1926. It was intended to celebrate the centenary of the death of George Frederick Handel with a festival at the Crystal Palace in 1859. To test the suitability of the palace a festival was held in 1857, two years before the centenary, featuring 2,000 singers and 386 instrumentalists conducted by Michael Costa. This first festival was an enormous success and more than 40,000 people attended, including Queen Victoria. The organ was built for the festival and subsequently enlarged so that by 1893 it had 4,394 pipes, 82 stops and four keyboards.

After the 1859 festival to celebrate the centenary of Handel's death, festivals were held there every three years. This photograph shows the honorary stewards for the festival in June 1926 with Capt. Young, Chairman of Penge Urban District Council, in the centre of the front row. August Manns, so long connected with the palace, was knighted in 1903.

The National Band Festival in the concert hall. The first brass band competition was held at the Crystal Palace in 1860, and was won by the Black Dyke Mills Band. However, it was not until the turn of the century that these annual contests became nationally important. Bands would travel from all over the country, and every spare room and hall in the district would be booked for practice.

The first important cricket match played at the Crystal Palace on 22 July 1864, between Kent and Nottinghamshire. In 1899 the Crystal Palace Company wrote to Dr W.G. Grace and suggested that he should become manager and secretary of a new club to be called London County. Grace, then in the twilight of his career, accepted the post. The cricket ground was enlarged and a new pavilion built. Grace employed a member of the Gloucestershire ground staff, Mr Murch, to be head groundsman. Grace would signal his approach when visiting the ground staff by blowing a whistle, as Murch was deaf and the others would be in a panic in case he hadn't heard the call. In 1909 Grace moved to a house at Mottingham called 'Fairmont', where he died six years later. He is buried at Elmers End.

The unveiling of the statue of George V at the Crystal Palace, 1913. Thomas Cook and Son, the occupiers of the building to the right of the statue, had a long association with the Crystal Palace, and one of the first 'Cook's Tours' was to the Great Exhibition.

A large group photograph outside the Crystal Palace. Obviously the group at the front became bored and started a card school!

The water chute, 1902.

The Jamaican court at the Colonial Exhibition, 1905.

The Crystal Palace has a close link with experiments into flight. One of the first ascents from the gardens was made in 1859 by Henry Coxwell, the Crystal Palace Company's official balloonist. Gas pipes were laid from the Sydenham gas works and regular flights were made with passengers and for scientific experiments. The balloon ground was near the north tower. Parachute drops were made from the balloons by young ladies in spangled costumes, and one, Leona Dare, ascended hanging by her teeth from a trapeze suspended under the basket.

The first English airship at the Crystal Palace. In June 1903 the first manned airship made an ascent from the Crystal Palace with Stanley Spencer, a noted balloonist, in control. Thereafter, many airship flights were made from the grounds and a special hangar was provided for the airship.

The first Aeronautical Exhibition was organized by the Aeronautical Society. It was opened in June 1868 and was an enormous success. Model flying machines were displayed. A model flying club was later formed at the Crystal Palace.

King George V and Queen Mary at the opening ceremony of the Festival of Empire, 12 May 1911.

In 1911, the year of King George's coronation, the Crystal Palace housed the Festival of Empire. Three-quarter size models of the parliament buildings of the Commonwealth were constructed and filled with exhibitions of the countries' produce. This is the Canadian parliament building.

An aerial view from over the low-level station. In the grounds are some of the Commonwealth buildings from the Festival of Empire of 1911, plus the round panorama building and Maxim's flying machine.

The Festival of Empire, 1911. The exhibition included a model of an Indian tea plantation, a Canadian logging camp and a South African diamond mine.

William Webster Hoare as the British chief in the Pageant of Empire, May 1911. More than 40,000 children visited to watch the performances.

North tower gardens. The cast-iron tank standing on columns, which fed this lake, held 193,000 gallons of water.

The topsy turvy railway. There was also a toboggan slide and a switchback railway. In 1888 there was a luminous cottage, which was painted inside with Balmain's luminous paint.

The north tower gardens and fairy archipelago at the time of the Festival of Empire, 1911. Attractions included the Eddystone Ride – 'the largest water chute on earth, each run 6d', the rapids – 'a thrilling trip through foaming torrents', and the electric canoes – 'a voyage on the lake through the marvellous grottos and caves, each trip 3d'. 'There was also a troupe of underwater swimmers, acrobats and 'ornamental swimmers'.

The fairy archipelago, Festival of Empire.

The electric canoes, Festival of Empire.

A miniature railway, named the All Red Route after the custom of colouring Empire and Commonwealth countries red on maps, took visitors round the show.

A view from the central balustrade. In 1911, despite the apparent success of the festival, the Crystal Palace Company was declared bankrupt. The palace was sold at auction. It was bought by the Duke of Plymouth for £230,000 to prevent the site from being developed by builders. The Lord Mayor of London started the King Edward National Memorial Fund, which bought the palace from the duke for the nation.

During the First World War, Crystal Palace was closed and became a naval barracks for up to 13,000 men. It was known formally as HMS *Victory VI* but was nicknamed HMS *Crystal Palace*.

The Royal Naval Volunteer Reserve war memorial, unveiled by the then Prince of Wales, 1931. This memorial is on a new site in the grounds today.

The Great Victory Exhibition was held at the Crystal Palace after the First World War and for a short time the Commonwealth, later the Imperial, War Museum, found a home here. In June 1920 the exhibition was officially opened by King George V.

The South London Exhibition of 1934, which attracted between 60,000 and 70,000 people in twelve days.

The Crystal Palace Co-operative Festival Display of July 1936. Maxim's flying machine is in the distance.

The South London Exhibition at the Crystal Palace, 1936. New Ideal Homesteads built many estates of houses in the area between the wars.

The Kensington Canine Society Championship Show, 1936. This photograph was taken a few months before the fatal fire.

The Upper Norwood Volunteer Fire Brigade, with its horse-drawn steam-powered pump. In 1866 fire broke out in the main building at 2.00 p.m. on a Sunday, when the palace was shut. Three men fought the blaze but it took hold and destroyed the north wing and north transept, including the natural history collections, royal apartments, library and printing office; they were never replaced – though insured, the amount was not sufficient to fund rebuilding. It is said that if the wind had been in a different direction the result might have been far worse. Indeed, seventy years later it was.

During the 1920s and '30s the Crystal Palace, under the general manager, Sir Henry Buckland, regained some of its appeal but could not regain fully its old glory. Concerts, dirt track racing, shows, dances and fireworks still continued. The south tower was used by John Logie Baird as a studio for his early experiments in television. Yearly attendances averaged a million, though it still closed on Sundays.

The Crystal Palace fire.

The centre transept soon after the outbreak of fire on 30 November 1936. Sir Henry Buckland was one of the first on the scene. Just after 7.00 p.m. Sir Henry and his daughter, Crystal, were passing the palace and saw a red glow. The alarm was raised but the small fire which had started in a staff toilet was fanned by a breeze, and raced through the tinder-dry timbers of the floor. Soon the whole building was ablaze.

The first fire brigade on the scene was from Penge, and they were soon joined by ninety fire-engines and five hundred firemen. The flames reached over 300 ft into the air and the glow could be seen for miles. Crowds flocked to the scene and mounted policemen were needed to clear the way for the fire crews. People stood on every hill in London to watch the blaze. It could be seen from as far away as Brighton and from a plane over the Channel. A BBC outside broadcast unit reported the fire as it happened and the fire brigade made a short film. Winston Churchill and the Duke of Kent visited the site. Churchill told a reporter: 'This is the end of an age.'

The building was a total loss. Lloyds paid the insurance of £200,000 – such a small sum that there could be no hope of rebuilding the palace. In the summer of 1937 the site was cleared, leaving only the towers standing.

The remains of the north nave.

The north nave, 1936. This picture was taken soon after the fire.

The towers were broken up in April 1941 and the scrap metal contributed to the war effort. The Crystal Palace was finally destroyed.

The Baird Television Company occupied this part of the palace and lost nearly all of the equipment in the laboratories and studios near the south tower.

During the Second World War the site was covered with rubble brought from areas of London destroyed during the Blitz. In April 1941 it was decided that the two towers were providing a landmark for the Luftwaffe. The north tower was destroyed by explosives, while the south tower was demolished brick by brick to avoid damage to nearby houses.